SUPERHERO BUNNY LEAGUE
SAVES THE WORLD!

Written and illustrated by

Jamie Smart

D1326649

Once upon a time, they were just normal bunnies …

OXFORD
UNIVERSITY PRESS

OXFORD
UNIVERSITY PRESS

Great Clarendon Street, Oxford, OX2 6DP, United Kingdom

Oxford University Press is a department of the University
of Oxford. It furthers the University's objective of excellence
in research, scholarship, and education by publishing
worldwide. Oxford is a registered trade mark of Oxford
University Press in the UK and in certain other countries

British Library Cataloguing in Publication Data
Data available

ISBN: 978-0-19-835656-1

10 9 8 7 6 5 4 3 2 1

Paper used in the production of this book is a natural, recyclable product
made from wood grown in sustainable forests. The manufacturing process
conforms to the environmental regulations of the country of origin.

Printed in China by Hing Yip

Acknowledgements

Series Advisor: Nikki Gamble

3

4

The next morning ...

Yawn!

STUMPY

Well, it's morning again.

I'm all ready for another boring day of being a rabbit.

Hang on, I can speak!

That's new!

B-b-b-b!

Blah! Blahhh!

People of Earth! I have taken over your televisions to give you an important message!

I have given all your bunny rabbits SUPER POWERS!

Erm ... accidentally.

Super powers?

How exciting! I wonder what my super powers are!

WHOOSH!

Maybe I can FLY, like that bunny!

Or lift heavy things, like that bunny!

Pfft! As if!

Or ...

Or ...

UNRAVEL!

YAH!

KITTENS!

Aw!

Kittens!

SHRINK!!

Amazing!

Derek grows huge when he's angry. Windy knows how to calm him down.

Wow! I wonder if I grow huge when I'm angry!

Ha ha!

I doubt it.

Well, you've made me feel a bit GRUMPY, so let's see what happens ...

YAH!

Argh!

Ha ha! You're too scared to be a hero!

I'll show you.

I'll find my super power!

But first ...

I'll need a cool outfit!

COSTUMES

COSTUMES

People of Earth!

Me again.

Huh?

Give me all your bunnies! I want the bunnies to work for ME!

All I have are silly robots.

Sorry, robots.

But SUPERBUNNIES?

Together, we could make chaos!

Moo ha ha!

I don't think so, Doctor Fuzzy-head!

Argh! Get off! Get off!

Betty's right, I AM special somehow.

I just need to find out how.

OK, here's a big empty field where no one can see me or laugh at me.

Now let's see ...

Maybe I'm SUPER FAST?

Puff!

Wheeze!

Nope!

Maybe I'm SUPER INTELLIGENT!

Wait, what was I thinking about?

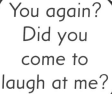

Welcome to Bunny HQ!

Where all the superbunnies live.

Superbunnies like YOU!

Are you the new superbunnies?

I ...

uh ...

Well, I'm Annabel, the chief science officer here at Bunny HQ.

You're ... beautiful!

Ignore him, Annabel. I'M the bunny you want. They call me HANDSOME STEVE.

Ah! New bunnies! Welcome to your new home!

HRRR!

Here at Bunny HQ, we will help you develop your super powers ...

He doesn't have any! Ha ha!

But Doctor Fuzzleglove's laser affected us ALL!

I, um.

I ...

Did I hear my name?

Gasp!

BUNNY-O-VISION

I am VERY angry with you bunnies.

Come out of there and be MY superbunnies!

Or I will set my ROBOTS upon you all! Moo ha ha!

BZZ!

BZZ!

Oi! Get away from my prize-winning carrot.

BUNNY HQ

SHUSH! I'm talking to the superbunnies.

I don't understand, how did you find our secret HQ?

The tracker ...

... which I planted on Stumpy's back!

Uh oh.

BOOP! BOOP! BOOP!

Stumpy!

You brought Doctor Fuzzleglove and his robots here?

I ... I ...

He has put us all at risk!

I ... I ...

Oh no! Today couldn't get any worse!

STAGGER!

TRIP!

BOOMF!!

Ha ha! He fell on his bottom!

No! Stop laughing at me!

HA! HA! HA!

NOOOOO!

23

GASP!

SPLOSH!

You got so embarrassed, you ...

turned into LIQUID!

This must be my super power!

I'm a LIQUID BUNNY!

Yes!

You know what to do, Stumpy!

Wait, do I?

Oh, YES!

They're taking their time.

BUNNY

SPLOOSH!

Whee!

My robots! Don't get them wet!

BZZ!

WHOOSH!

BZZ!

BZZ!

Whee!

Electricity and liquids don't mix!

SPLOSH!

Now it's your turn, Doctor!

Eek! Not likely!

25

GROO!

Woo! Go, Stumpy!

I still have a secret weapon – SUPER-ABSORBENT PAPER TOWELS!

RIIIIP!

Gasp! My weakness!

Stand aside, Stumpy! We'll show him what to do with his paper towels!

No! Get away!

WRAP! WRAP! WRAP!

SWING!

Have a nice flight, Doctor Fuzzy-head!

FLING!

BOMF!

Mmf!

BWOOOOOOOOP!

Oh no! I'm changing back!

SPLAT!

That was amazing, Stumpy!

Well, I need to work on my landing!

You're a hero!

A ... hero?

Three cheers for Stumpy!

Hip ... hip ... HOORAY!

Hop ... hop ... HOORAY!

Hip ... hip ... HOORAY!

Sorry I was such a bully, dude. Can I join your team?

My ... team?

Indeed! Since you four all work so well together ...

Stumpy, you will lead the ...